AN IDEAS INTO ACTION GUIDEBOOK

Broadening Your Organizational Perspective

IDEAS INTO ACTION GUIDEBOOKS

Aimed at managers and executives who are concerned with their own and others' development, each guidebook in this series gives specific advice on how to complete a developmental task or solve a leadership problem.

LEAD CONTRIBUTOR	Ellen Van Velsor
CONTRIBUTORS	Jennifer Martineau, Russ McCallian, Bertrand Sereno, Sandrine Tunezerwe, Sophia Zhao
DIRECTOR OF ASSESSMENTS, TOOLS, AND PUBLICATIONS	Sylvester Taylor
MANAGER, PUBLICATION DEVELOPMENT	Peter Scisco
EDITORS	Stephen Rush Karen Lewis
ASSOCIATE EDITOR	Shaun Martin
COPY EDITOR	Tammie McLean
WRITER	Martin Wilcox
DESIGN AND LAYOUT	Joanne Ferguson
COVER DESIGN	Laura J. Gibson Chris Wilson, 29 & Company
RIGHTS AND PERMISSIONS	Kelly Lombardino

CCL No. 456
ISBN No. 978-1-60491-158-9

CENTER FOR CREATIVE LEADERSHIP
POST OFFICE BOX 26300
GREENSBORO, NORTH CAROLINA 27438-6300
336-288-7210
WWW.CCL.ORG / PUBLICATIONS

Broadening Your Organizational Perspective

Ellen Van Velsor

Center for
Creative
Leadership

www.ccl.org

THE IDEAS INTO ACTION GUIDEBOOK SERIES

This series of guidebooks draws on the practical knowledge that the Center for Creative Leadership (CCL) has generated since its inception in 1970. The purpose of the series is to provide leaders with specific advice on how to complete a developmental task or solve a leadership challenge. In doing that, the series carries out CCL's mission to advance the understanding, practice, and development of leadership for the benefit of society worldwide.

CCL's unique position as a research and education organization supports a community of accomplished scholars and educators in a community of shared knowledge. CCL's knowledge community holds certain principles in common, and its members work together to understand and generate practical responses to the ever-changing circumstances of leadership and organizational challenges.

In its interactions with a richly varied client population, in its research into the effect of leadership on organizational performance and sustainability, and in its deep insight into the workings of organizations, CCL creates new, sound ideas that leaders all over the world put into action every day. We believe you will find the Ideas Into Action Guidebooks an important addition to your leadership toolkit.

Table of Contents

7 The Challenges of Advancement

8 What Stops You

14 What Helps You: Learning

20 What Helps You: A Variety of Challenging Experiences

30 Conclusion

31 Background

32 Suggested Resources

In Brief

As a manager, you may seek to advance within your organization, to move upward and to take on additional levels of responsibility in order to gain personal rewards and achieve greater organizational results. However, advancing can be tricky. The most effective way to do it is to gain a broad organizational perspective that allows you to see beyond your own functional area and to understand how other areas interrelate and support the organization.

First, you must seek out the things that are holding you back, such as organizational or personal forces. For instance, an organization can hold individuals back by developing them in a stovepipe and limiting their opportunities for expanding their perspective. Or an individual may have an extremely limited view of career advancement, and only seek to move upward rather than gain experience across the organization.

To combat these negative forces, you should seek out learning opportunities and challenging experiences. By learning about other areas in your organization and participating in challenging experiences that broaden your horizons and push you out of your comfort zone, you can gain a broad perspective that will allow you to successfully advance as a leader.

The Challenges of Advancement

If you're like most managers, you want to advance: to take on more responsibility at a higher level in your organization. Personal rewards and the opportunity to achieve greater organizational results are strong inducements. But advancing can be tricky, even for very successful managers.

CCL has studied what drives the advancement of executives, and has learned that perhaps the most important element is having a broad organizational perspective—that is, being able to see beyond your own functional area and understanding how other functional areas interrelate and support the organization.

Furthermore, having a narrow functional orientation can lead to derailment. A promotion might take you beyond your current level of competence. You may be unable to manage in a different department, you may not know how to handle management outside of your current function, or you might not understand how other departments function within the organization.

Broadening your organizational perspective is not a quick-fix activity. It requires reflection, judgment, planning, and time. But

you can quickly gain an understanding of what is required that will eventually take you where you want to go. This guidebook will help you do that.

Throughout this guidebook you will find assessments and worksheets you can use in the effort to broaden your organizational perspective.

The assessments will provide information to assist you in understanding your challenges, and the worksheets will facilitate your choosing and prioritizing actions. As we cover key components of your perspective-broadening work, we will refer you to the appropriate sheet and tell you how to use it.

Before you can begin taking action, however, you must take note of the things that stop you. Not surprisingly, both organizational and personal forces play a role, and your past successes and the strengths that propelled them are factors in both of these types of forces. Broadening your organizational view is thus largely a question of acquiring a variety of experiences and learning from them.

What Stops You

The forces that hinder your developing a broader view are organizational—the policies and practices of your organization—and personal—your beliefs and understandings about who you are and what you believe to be true.

Organizational Forces

Your organization can hinder your ability to develop the broad organizational perspective needed to be successful. Primarily, the organization does this by

- developing individuals in a stovepipe or silo—allowing them to make small vertical moves in a single functional area (providing people with more of the same)
- moving people too quickly through jobs in another functional area
- failing to give effective feedback
- punishing failure without providing the opportunity to learn

Stovepipes and silos. Many organizations see moving managers out of their current functional area as a major risk. They are reluctant to gamble a known quantity—your skill and performance—for the chance that your ability will translate to added value in a different functional area. It's much easier and less risky to keep people where they are and move them up in a narrow channel.

> Kelly was an exceptional salesperson who was able to meet her quota year after year. Though she wanted to get into product marketing, the organization believed it needed her in sales. Whenever Kelly mentioned her desire to try product marketing, the organization reminded her of her success in sales and how much they appreciated the work she had done. She pressed further about moving to product marketing, but her superiors became firmer, stating that she was needed in sales. To keep her focused on staying in the sales channel, the organization made sure she was appropriately compensated, and offered her larger territories with more prestigious accounts and a title with more senior-level status. Later in her career Kelly went on to become a sales manager and then a sales director. When the position of vice president of sales and marketing became available, a position Kelly really wanted, the organization disregarded her, believing that she did not have the product-marketing skills necessary to do the job.

Quick movement. Many organizations offer managers rotational assignments in order for them to get experience in other functional areas. Unfortunately, managers often move through those assignments so quickly that they never get to learn from the experience.

Yuri was hired as a production assistant, and because of his educational background and prior experience, the organization put him on the fast track. This included brief stints on the production line and in maintenance, scheduling, and quality control. None of Yuri's assignments lasted longer than a year. As a result of these short stints, he never had the opportunity to see the effects of his decisions, nor did he fully grasp any of the organization's processes and their relationships to each other. When Yuri was made director of manufacturing, he made numerous costly mistakes that dramatically affected his facility's production.

Feedback failure. Many organizations don't do a good job of giving people specific feedback that they can act upon. People tend to receive vague feedback based solely on their results instead of on the process used to reach the results.

Hong Mei's abrasive style served her well in the call center. Though she had a high turnover rate among employees, she nonetheless had the results, she thought, to justify her behavior. In fact, the organization often gave her feedback describing her as a producer, a real results-oriented individual. After being promoted several times, she was suddenly and unexpectedly called into her boss's office and told she was being let go. Her direct reports could no longer stand her abrasiveness. Hong Mei never knew what had happened or how.

Failure without learning. Many organizations want individuals to be risk takers and to think more creatively. Often, however, when someone takes risks and fails, the organization's response is to demote, fire, or otherwise leave that individual feeling like a failure.

Richard's superiors gave him the task of managing the package redesign of the company's flagship product. Richard and his team spent weeks conducting marketing surveys, meeting with focus groups, and working with design firms. When the new product came out, it was an abject failure. The corporation lost a lot of money and damaged its image with customers, so they reintroduced the old packaging. Everyone above Richard had agreed to the new packaging, but only Richard was fired.

Personal Forces

Your organization plays a major role in determining whether you will be able to develop a broad organizational perspective, but you also play a key role. Developing a broader organizational perspective requires a fundamental shift in what you may view as advancing your career. Many leaders view career advancement as climbing the corporate ladder, moving only upward along the organization's hierarchy. To develop a broad organizational perspective, you need to shift that view to accommodate not just upward movement but also lateral and possibly even downward movement.

This shift in view takes courage. You have to temper the ambition that often pushes you to move upward. You have to deal with peers or bosses who believe only in the traditional view of advancement or an organizational culture that views mainly upward movement within function as valuable. You have to recognize that even if you develop this broad organizational perspective, you have no guarantee that it will be rewarded. And finally, you have to overcome the fear of appearing inadequate or incompetent when trying something new in a different functional area.

In addition, other behaviors can hinder your development. You may rely too much on strengths or previously successful strategies, ignore a fatal flaw, avoid untested areas or challenges, or focus on one type of work.

Overreliance on strengths. Too much success can be a bad thing. Managers can develop too narrow a functional orientation by having only continued success in a single area, such as sales, manufacturing, or research. They risk the possibility of derailing when the situation requires a broader organizational perspective.

Your strengths have helped you achieve your current level of success, but CCL research has shown that any strength can become a weakness. For instance:

- If you're persevering (no matter what it takes, you get it done), you can become stubborn (never giving up even when it's obvious you're facing a no-win situation).
- If you're principled (you believe that certain values must guide the way you operate), you can become unbending (failing to consider the uniqueness of a situation).
- If you're optimistic (you always look for the upside of a situation), you can become impractical (not recognizing the reality of a situation).
- If you're trusting (you believe people will do the right thing), you can become gullible (letting people take advantage of you).
- If you're methodical (you always approach problems with a systematic process), you can become rigid (seeing things one way and only one way).
- If you're persuasive (you're able to convince people to see things your way), you can become pressuring (making people feel as if they are not being heard).

There are many other examples. The point is that overusing your strengths, whatever they may be, can lead to your greatest strength becoming your greatest weakness. By relying too much on your strengths, you hinder your ability to develop other, more appropriate strengths for any situation.

Because developing a broad organizational perspective involves learning to deal with very different situations, you need to develop strengths relevant for each specific situation. The following examples demonstrate what happens when individuals fail to develop multiple strengths.

Ignoring a flaw. After Jason was promoted to plant manager, his company was bought by a larger international company. As part of the change, the larger company expected its employees to adhere to its cultural norms. Unfortunately, Jason ignored this feedback. He continued to practice the same behaviors that he had used in his old company, such as storming into meetings, using inappropriate language, and consistently pressing his management for quick answers to problems. All of these actions ran counter to the new organizational culture, which emphasized respectful interactions, deferring to authority, and waiting for superiors to make decisions. The company tolerated Jason for as long as it took to find a replacement.

Avoiding untested areas. Wendy had risen very rapidly in the investment division of the organization even though she knew very little about finance. To counter her inadequacy, she relied on people who had strong financial backgrounds. Wendy rationalized that avoiding financial knowledge would help her because having it would only get in the way of managing processes that supported the investment division. Others began to note her lack of knowledge, and when Wendy and one of her direct reports applied for the same position, management gave the direct report the opportunity.

Focusing on one type of work. Heidi graduated at the top of her engineering school class and took a job as an engineering assistant in the maintenance management department of a coal mine. In that department she held various positions that involved her obtaining greater technical knowledge of the long-wall mining system. Though she had opportunities in surveying, union relations, and the prep facility, she chose to continue working on the long-wall system, developing expertise in keeping those machines working through two shifts. She eventually became shift manager and then production manager for the line. When the position of supervisor for the entire mine came open, she believed she would be a logical fit because, in her mind, no one understood mining operations better than she did. The organization saw things differently. They wanted someone who had a variety of experiences that would support new organizational initiatives, and chose someone else.

Note a common thread running through all of the above examples: the inability to learn, to take a risk, and to be challenged by something new hindered the development of a broad organizational perspective.

What Helps You: Learning

Although broadening your organizational perspective will depend significantly on having a variety of challenging experiences, especially in functions other than the one you are currently working in, just having experiences doesn't guarantee that you will learn from them. Before you seek challenges, you need to make sure your learning skills will serve you well. It may not always be possible for you to change your function, but it is possible to become a better learner.

To become better at learning from experiences, you should first examine your willingness to learn, your ability to learn, and your learning versatility.

Willingness to Learn

The first step in becoming better at learning from experience is to reflect on your willingness to learn: whether you want to engage in a new experience and to what level you are willing to commit to that experience. New experiences provoke such emotions as fear of inadequacy, anger and frustration over not doing something right, and anxiety about failing. Your willingness to learn relates to how well you deal with these kinds of emotions. People who do not manage these emotions well have a low tolerance for risk and so have less willingness to learn.

In order to get a better understanding of your willingness, you need to understand the anatomy of a learning experience. See the sidebar, Anatomy of a Learning Experience, which outlines the stages, the progression of experiences, and feelings that individuals develop when learning something new.

In order to improve your willingness to learn, you must recognize the emotions that will occur when you are going against your grain, acknowledge those emotions as a necessary part of doing something new, and accept that your performance may suffer in the short term. However, in the long term you will benefit from improved performance and a broader understanding.

Ability to Learn

Once you have determined your willingness to learn, the next step is to examine your ability to learn. You need to consider the extent to which you seek and use feedback, learn from mistakes, and are open to criticism.

Understanding your ability to learn isn't easy to do. You have to be willing to be vulnerable without being defensive. It requires a commitment to improve your self-awareness, which will help you approach new experiences with a broader perspective and help determine what is key in order for you to learn from the experience. One way to do this is to use your current strengths—the skills and talents you successfully use every day—when attempting to learn something new.

Anatomy of a Learning Experience

Stage 1: Comfort zone. When you are in your comfort zone, you are going with your grain, using your existing skills and feeling comfortable about how you use them.

Stage 2: Potential learning event. In order for you to learn, you have to have an opportunity to learn. It is through challenges that you begin to become conscious of the areas in which you are not yet competent.

Stage 3: Going against your grain. When you are going against your grain, you are in the process of learning. You are out of your comfort zone, which causes you to experience a performance drop. This performance drop creates a range of emotions that test your willingness to learn. Such emotions occur in the workplace every time you take on a new responsibility; they cause the knot in your stomach that wakes you in the middle of the night with the thought "I don't know if I can do this." During this period, you become conscious of your lack of competence.

Stage 4: Returning to the comfort zone or reaping the benefits. For some people, the range of feelings exposed by a drop in performance is too much to handle. As a result, they return to their comfort zone and continue to use their existing skills. But if you continue to go against your grain, what was once uncomfortable eventually becomes comfortable. As a result of turning this corner, your performance increases at a significant rate, and you become conscious of what it takes to make you more competent.

Stage 5: New comfort zone. Sooner or later your performance levels off to a new comfort zone, and you are no longer conscious of what you need to do to be competent. Instead, at this higher performance level, you do what you need to do at an unconscious level as part of your repertoire of learned skills. You have achieved this learning gain by having the willingness to go against your grain.

For example, let's say that being analytical is one of your strengths. You like to break things down step by step. Once you recognize this strength, you can use it to increase your ability to learn from new experiences.

Let's explore the notion of increasing your self-awareness through getting a better understanding of your strengths. When you ask people about their strengths and how they acquired them, you're likely to hear one of two answers: either that the strength came naturally or that they consciously or unconsciously developed it in response to a situation. If you were to ask those people how they know that these abilities are actually strengths, they might give examples in which they successfully used them and in which others recognized their success. The notion of strengths is often tied to success. When people describe the strength of persistence, for example, they might talk about situations in which they successfully accomplished tasks in spite of tremendous barriers and setbacks.

Learning Versatility

The third step to understanding yourself as a learner is to recognize your learning style—the tactics that you use. You can then figure out how to broaden your tactics to make sure you learn the most from your experiences.

Each of us has a preferred learning tactic we use more often than others. Think of how well each of these tactics describes you:

- When you get a new software package, you get really excited and anxious about using it and you recognize those feelings in yourself.
- When you get a new software package, you open it up, install it on your computer, and work your way through it. If you get stuck, you might look at the manual.
- When you get a new software package, you read the instructions and make sure you understand them before you install the software.

- When you get a new software package, you ask your colleagues if they know about it or have tried it. When you run into trouble, you don't think twice about calling the toll-free number or asking somebody else for help.

Probably one of these tactics—feeling, taking action, thinking, and accessing others—resonates more for you than the others, which may mean that you are relying too much on that tactic. These learning tactics are not mutually exclusive, but most of us have a preference or natural inclination toward one or another. Complete Assessment 1: Learning Tactic Checklist to get a sense of your preferred learning tactic.

There is no one correct learning tactic. As you look over your responses to the learning tactic checklist, remember that the risk is not in failing to choose the right tactic, but in overusing or misusing a particular tactic. For example, if you overuse taking action without accessing others, you risk repeating someone else's work or not getting the support you need to fully learn from the experience. If you overuse thinking without taking action, you miss the learning that can occur from experience. The goal is to become a multifaceted learner, adept at learning in various ways depending on the situation. The most successful learners are able to use a wider variety of tactics more often.

The choice of learning tactics happens experience by experience. A more versatile learning style is an integral component of developing a broader organizational perspective. Consider the following example: You have been in charge of sales for years, relying on a handshake and personal visits with tremendous success. The company shifts to a new technology-based marketing approach that substitutes databases and mailing lists, areas in which you are unskilled, for the personal visits that you prefer. From this example, let's look at how drawing on all the learning types can create a developmental experience and broaden your organizational perspective.

Assessment 1: Learning Tactic Checklist

Check the statements that best complete the prompt for you.

When I am faced with a challenging opportunity…

Statement	✓	Tactic
I carefully consider how I feel.		feeling
I confront myself if I am avoiding the work challenge.		feeling
I carefully consider how others might feel.		feeling
I trust my feelings about what to do.		feeling
I acknowledge the impact of my feelings on what I decide to do.		feeling
I figure it out by trial and error.		taking action
I allow my own experience to be my guide.		taking action
I immerse myself in the situation to figure it out quickly.		taking action
I don't allow lack of information or input to keep me from making my move.		taking action
I commit myself to making something happen.		taking action
I regularly access magazine articles, books, or the Internet to gain knowledge or information.		thinking
I ask myself, "How is this similar to other things I know?"		thinking
I imagine how different opinions might play out.		thinking
I try to conceptualize what the ideal person would do.		thinking
I try to mentally rehearse my actions before entering the situation.		thinking
I often seek the advice of those around me.		accessing others
I look for role models and try to emulate the behavior of those people.		accessing others
I find someone who can give me feedback about how I am doing.		accessing others
I look for a course or training experience.		accessing others
I look for someone who has had experience in that area.		accessing others

Look back at the tactics you've checked. The tactic with the most check marks is likely to be your preferred learning tactic.

Note. Adapted from *Becoming a More Versatile Learner*, by M. A. Dalton, 1998.

- **Feeling:** Acknowledge the emotional impact of the change—the feelings of loss, uncertainty, and anxiety it creates in you.
- **Taking action:** Tackle the new technology head-on—begin using it, tinkering with it, making mistakes, and finding out how to do with it what you used to do personally.
- **Thinking:** Research how to use the technology and identify its advantages and disadvantages. Draft a plan to transition into the new methodology.
- **Accessing others:** Talk to other individuals who have made a similar transition. Research how other organizations have shifted from a personal approach to database technology.

The breadth of learning types and whether you choose to apply them determine whether the outcome of the experience is developmental and tends to broaden your skill base, or if you avoid learning from the experience and therefore narrow your set of skills.

What Helps You: A Variety of Challenging Experiences

With a solid understanding of and commitment to learning, you can find challenging experiences to broaden your organizational perspective. These experiences can come in the context of new job assignments, activities within your current job, or activities outside of your job, such as volunteer work.

In some cases you have flexibility in choosing job assignments. If so, you can develop a broad organizational perspective by choosing assignments that offer the greatest opportunity to learn. Without such flexibility, you may have to find creative ways to develop a broad organizational perspective. This may include finding short-term job-related assignments, making sure you get as much feedback as possible on the work you are doing now, finding role models and coaches who can share what they've learned, training and reading, and taking on assignments outside of work, such as community service or other kinds of volunteer activities.

Whatever the situation, the key component to learning from an experience is that the experience is challenging. What is a challenging experience? CCL has identified five challenging, developmental situations that can help you in gaining a broad organizational perspective: experiencing a job transition, creating change, managing at high levels of responsibility, managing boundaries, and dealing with diversity.

How can you use these components so that they contribute to broadening your organizational perspective? Keeping in mind that an experience in any of these categories must be challenging to be valuable, let's walk through the steps to create a plan for developing a broader organizational perspective.

Step 1: **Assess where you are and where you want to go.** To prioritize which challenges to tackle, first identify which management skills are your strengths and understand how the organization defines a broad organizational perspective. To do this, you should

- reflect on your own assessment of your current strengths and consider what is necessary to reach the next level of what you define as successfully becoming broader in your organizational perspective
- reflect on the feedback that has been provided to you by both superiors and direct reports

Use Worksheet 1: Managerial Abilities Evaluation to explore your organization's and your concepts of what a broad organizational perspective means.

Worksheet 1: Managerial Abilities Evaluation

Consider the following managerial abilities. If you consider an ability to be one of your strengths, label it *S* in the second column; if a weakness, label it *W*. Based on conversations with your boss and others, determine whether each managerial ability is important for developing a broad organizational perspective. Use the third column to label it *I* for important or *U* for unimportant.

Managerial Ability	Strength or Weakness?	Important or Unimportant?
1. Acting with flexibility: behaving in ways that are often seen as opposites, such as being both tough and compassionate or leading and allowing others to lead.		
2. Being a quick study: quickly mastering new technical and business knowledge.		
3. Building and mending relationships: developing and maintaining positive relationships with coworkers and external parties.		
4. Comfort with ambiguity: responding when information is incomplete, conditions are changing, or the future is uncertain.		
5. Compassion and sensitivity: showing genuine interest in others and sensitivity to their needs.		
6. Confronting problem employees: acting decisively and with fairness in dealing with problem employees.		
7. Creating systems: building systems to control work processes and facilitate the management of day-to-day operations at lower levels.		
8. Dealing with conflict: addressing conflict in an appropriate way for the situation by reducing it or avoiding it.		
9. Decisiveness: being quick and approximate rather than slow and precise in many management situations.		

Managerial Ability	Strength or Weakness?	Important or Unimportant?
10. Hiring talented staff: recognizing talent and recruiting the best people.		
11. Leading employees: directing and motivating staff.		
12. Perseverance: accomplishing goals in the face of obstacles.		
13. Problem solving: finding solutions to problems through careful analysis and application of new approaches.		
14. Putting people at ease: displaying warmth and a good sense of humor.		
15. Self-awareness: accurately assessing your strengths and weaknesses.		
16. Setting a developmental climate: developing employees by providing challenge and opportunity.		
17. Straightforwardness and composure: being steadfast, reliable, and honest in difficult situations.		
18. Taking charge of your career: recognizing career goals and planning a course of action for achieving those goals.		
19. Taking responsibility: handling situations in which you are completely responsible and accountable.		
20. Thinking strategically: rising above the day-to-day issues and taking a broader perspective that is more organizationally focused and oriented to the future.		
21. Work team orientation: accomplishing tasks by managing others.		
22. Working with executives: presenting to, persuading, and building productive relationships with higher management.		

Step 2: Find areas to develop that the organization says are important for obtaining a broad organizational perspective. Transfer your information from Worksheet 1 to the appropriate quadrants of Worksheet 2: Importance in Developing a Broad Organizational Perspective.

Worksheet 2: Importance in Developing a Broad Organizational Perspective

Write the number of each managerial ability from Worksheet 1 in the appropriate quadrant below. For example, if you consider number 1 a strength and the organization considers it unimportant, write 1 in the upper left quadrant.

Unimportant for developing broad perspectives and a strength (Abilities I put as an *S* and the organization had as a *U*)	Important for developing broad perspectives and a strength (Abilities I put as an *S* and the organization had as an *I*)
Unimportant for developing broad perspectives and a weakness (Abilities I put as a *W* and the organization had as a *U*)	Important for developing broad perspectives and a weakness (Abilities I put as a *W* and the organization had as an *I*)

Consider the groupings you have made. Note particularly the items located in the bottom right quadrant—important and a weakness. These are potential starting points for a development plan geared to achieving a broader organizational perspective.

The analysis you just completed isn't static. What's important for success in your organization may change over time. You should revisit this list once every six months, or during performance appraisals, to make sure it's current with your company's view. What does stay the same is the process of identifying the gaps between your skills and those necessary for success. To carry out that process, you need self-awareness and the help of others.

Step 3: Find ways to build skills. After identifying which of the managerial skills you want to develop, you need to find challenging experiences to help you develop those skills. Based on CCL's research, there are a number of categories of job components that contribute to building skills. In Assessment 2: Managerial Abilities and Developmental Job Components, we have listed managerial abilities, and for each have given examples of developmental job components that can help you build those skills. You can use this assessment to reflect on which developmental job components might be best and available for you in your current situation, given the managerial abilities you wish to develop.

Then use Assessment 3: Choosing Specific Assignments to identify specific assignments that could help to create the developmental challenges you need to broaden your perspective.

With a solid understanding of and commitment to learning, you can find challenging experiences to broaden your organizational perspective.

Assessment 2: Managerial Abilities and Developmental Job Components

Consider the managerial abilities you wish to develop and their developmental job components. In the third column, check the components that would be best for you. In the fourth column, check the ones that are available.

Managerial Ability	Developmental Job Components	Best Components	Available Components
1. Acting with flexibility	Unfamiliar responsibilities High stakes Work across cultures		
2. Being a quick study	Unfamiliar responsibilities New directions High stakes External pressure Influence without authority Work across cultures		
3. Building and mending relationships	Unfamiliar responsibilities New directions Inherited problems External pressure Influence without authority Work across cultures		
4. Comfort with ambiguity	Unfamiliar responsibilities Scope and scale		
5. Compassion and sensitivity	Problems with employees Work group diversity		
6. Confronting problem employees	Inherited problems Problems with employees		
7. Creating systems	New directions Scope and scale Work across cultures		

Managerial Ability	Developmental Job Components	Best Components	Available Components
8. Dealing with conflict	External pressure Influence without authority Work group diversity		
9. Decisiveness	High stakes Scope and scale		
10. Hiring talented staff	New directions Scope and scale		
11. Leading employees	New directions Inherited problems Problems with employees Work group diversity		
12. Perseverance	Inherited problems High stakes Scope and scale External pressure		
13. Problem solving	Unfamiliar responsibilities New directions Inherited problems Influence without authority Work across cultures Work group diversity		
14. Putting people at ease	External pressure Influence without authority		
15. Self-awareness	Unfamiliar responsibilities Work across cultures		
16. Setting a developmental climate	Inherited problems Problems with employees Work group diversity		
17. Straightforwardness and composure	High stakes Scope and scale External pressure Influence without authority Work group diversity		

Managerial Ability	Developmental Job Components	Best Components	Available Components
18. Taking charge of your career	Unfamiliar responsibilities Work across cultures		
19. Taking responsibility	New directions Problems with employees High stakes		
20. Thinking strategically	New directions Inherited problems Scope and scale		
21. Work team orientation	Problems with employees Scope and scale		
22. Working with executives	New directions Scope and scale External pressure Influence without authority		

Assessment 3: Choosing Specific Assignments

In Assessment 2, you determined the developmental job components that are best and available for you. Locate them below, and check specific assignments you could complete to broaden your perspective.

Developmental Job Components	Specific Assignments
Unfamiliar responsibilities	❏ Take on a colleague's job. ❏ Learn new technology and teach it to others. ❏ Serve on a task force dealing with a new issue. ❏ Volunteer in a nonprofit agency. ❏ Do a job rotation in a different business function.
New directions	❏ Reorganize a system in response to customer demands. ❏ Develop a new mission statement. ❏ Develop a five-year business plan. ❏ Serve on a reengineering team. ❏ Oversee construction of a new facility. ❏ Launch a new product.

Developmental Job Components	Specific Assignments
Inherited problems	❏ Work with a dissatisfied customer or supplier. ❏ Supervise a cost-cutting initiative. ❏ Manage an under-resourced project. ❏ Supervise liquidation of a project or product. ❏ Troubleshoot a flawed product or system.
Problems with employees	❏ Teach a class to a resistant audience. ❏ Resolve a conflict between yourself and a colleague or subordinate. ❏ Coach an employee with a development problem. ❏ Train new employees.
High stakes	❏ Manage the visit of a VIP. ❏ Make a presentation to the board of directors. ❏ Set challenging and visible goals for your group. ❏ Negotiate a mission-critical contract. ❏ Manage an event that was previously a success. ❏ Serve on a high-visibility task force.
Scope and scale	❏ Serve on multiple project teams. ❏ Pursue an advanced degree while maintaining your current job. ❏ Assume additional responsibilities following downsizing. ❏ Broaden the services or products currently offered by your group.
External pressure	❏ Answer customer complaints. ❏ Make speeches. ❏ Exhibit at a trade show booth. ❏ Negotiate with external stakeholders. ❏ Serve as a liaison to another organization. ❏ Lobby for the organization.
Influence without authority	❏ Present a proposal to top management. ❏ Become active in a professional organization. ❏ Work on a community or political committee. ❏ Do a project across functions.
Work across cultures	❏ Take a business trip to a foreign country. ❏ Host visitors from another country. ❏ Manage a multinational project. ❏ Serve as an overseas liaison.

Developmental Job Components	Specific Assignments
Work group diversity	❏ Create an internship position in your group to bring in diverse students. ❏ Join a community group focusing on diversity. ❏ Hire and develop people of different genders, races, and ethnic groups. ❏ Train in your group's diversity program.

You can find more examples of jobs and job assignments that might match your development needs in the following CCL publications: *Eighty-Eight Assignments for Development in Place: Enhancing the Developmental Challenge of Existing Jobs* and *Developmental Assignments: Creating Learning Experiences without Changing Jobs*. In addition, CCL's Job Challenge Profile guides the learner through a process of matching jobs and job assignments with needs.

Conclusion

To broaden your organizational perspective, identify and participate in a variety of experiences that your organization values, and make sure you can learn from them. Doing that takes time and planning, but that's how you position yourself to move up as a more effective leader.

Combining challenges with the ability to learn gives you the opportunity to gain a wider perspective on your own leadership strengths and development needs, and frees you from seeing advancement in strictly vertical terms. Rather, you will be able to see how to enhance your experience and advance your learning through moving horizontally, advancing not just your career, but your overall leadership abilities. Furthermore, having a wider perspective not only enhances your opportunities for advancement, but also improves your resilience and ability to adapt to an increasingly turbulent organizational world. It provides you with more personal resources that you can apply to the changes that no one can predict but everyone knows are coming.

Background

The Center for Creative Leadership has conducted extensive research on derailment—contrasting those people who make it to the top with those who derail. These studies have identified characteristics that mark the difference between managers who continue to be considered highly promotable and those who leave the organization involuntarily or reach a plateau. This research has been subsequently confirmed by data from Benchmarks, CCL's comprehensive 360-degree assessment tool that identifies strengths and development needs, encourages and guides change, and offers strategic insights for middle to upper-middle managers and executives.

CCL has also done a great deal of work on learning. For instance, it has found that individuals who report using all of the learning tactics (feeling, taking action, thinking, accessing others) more than the average are also more likely to report engaging in challenging opportunities and seeking and using feedback. The results of this work can be seen in the Learning Tactics Inventory (Jossey-Bass/Pfeiffer) and in the CCL guidebook *Becoming a More Versatile Learner*. (The tactics themselves build on the work of a number of learning theorists: for example, Reg Revans on action learning, Donald Meichenbaum on cognitive rehearsal, and Albert Bandura on social learning and learning from direct experience. The work on the feeling tactics was informed by the neoanalytic work of Karen Horney.)

CCL's work on the idea that individuals who are better learners will become better managers can be found in the books

The Lessons of Experience (Lexington Books, 1988) and *Breaking the Glass Ceiling*. It can also be found in the CCL report *Learning How to Learn from Experience: Impact of Stress and Coping*.

The three dimensions of willingness to learn, ability to learn, and learning variety are drawn from CCL research and reflected in the learning assessment tool Prospector.

Suggested Resources

Dalton, M. A. (1998). *Becoming a more versatile learner*. Greensboro, NC: Center for Creative Leadership.

Lombardo, M. M., & Eichinger, R. W. (1989). *Eighty-eight assignments for development in place: Enhancing the developmental challenge of existing jobs*. Greensboro, NC: Center for Creative Leadership.

Lombardo, M. M., & Eichinger, R. W. (1989). *Preventing derailment: What to do before it's too late*. Greensboro, NC: Center for Creative Leadership.

McCauley, C. (2006). *Developmental assignments: Creating learning experiences without changing jobs*. Greensboro, NC: Center for Creative Leadership.

McCauley, C., Ohlott, P., & Ruderman, M. (1999). *Job challenge profile, facilitator's guide: Learning from work experience*. San Francisco, CA: Jossey-Bass.

Van Velsor, E., & Leslie, J. B. (1996). *A look at derailment today: North America and Europe*. Greensboro, NC: Center for Creative Leadership.

Ordering Information

TO GET MORE INFORMATION, TO ORDER OTHER IDEAS INTO ACTION GUIDEBOOKS, OR TO FIND OUT ABOUT BULK-ORDER DISCOUNTS, PLEASE CONTACT US BY PHONE AT 336-545-2810 OR VISIT OUR ONLINE BOOKSTORE AT WWW.CCL.ORG/GUIDEBOOKS.